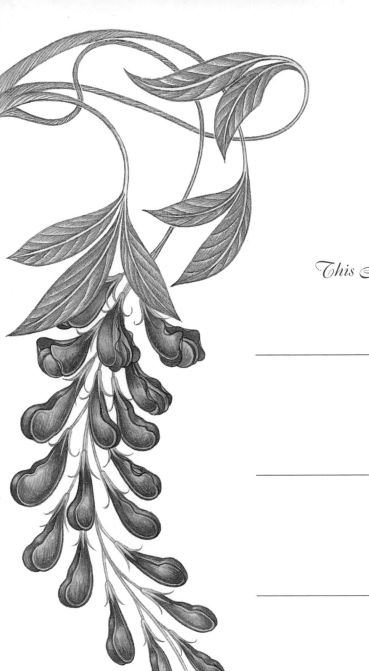

This Book was given to

_____

by

_____

on

_____

Giving Voice to Myself

A Memory Book for Women

Watercolors by Claudia Karabaic Sargent

Text by Peg Streep

A BULFINCH PRESS BOOK

LITTLE, BROWN AND COMPANY

Boston   New York   Toronto   London

*W*e are so many selves. It's not just the long-ago child within us who needs tenderness and inclusion, but the person we were last year, wanted to be yesterday, tried to become.

. . . *W*hat brings together these ever-shifting selves of infinite reactions and returnings is this: There is always one true inner voice.

— *Gloria Steinem*

*W*ith my singing I can make
A refuge for my spirit's sake,
A house of shining words . . .

— *Sara Teasdale*

About This Journal

Created by two women, *Giving Voice to Myself* is a journal especially for women. It has a simple premise: that life is not a journey from one point to another, but, instead, one animated by the relationship of the past to the present, the present to the future. We find ourselves and our voices not just in the women we are today but in the children and adolescents we once were and in the human beings we will become tomorrow. We find ourselves in recollection and in understanding, in looking forward and in questioning. This journal recognizes too that the "self" cannot be described geometrically, that we cannot draw a circle with a compass and label it "me." The self is instead more like a pomegranate or peony, filled with seeds of promise or overlapping petals around a center. For a woman to give voice to herself is to sing a mosaic of many songs — the songs of daughter and sister, lover and friend, mother and worker, of joy and optimism, of sorrow and pain. It is a voice, too, that, like the body from which it emanates, changes over time.

We hope you use this book as the place either to record your own thoughts over time, to express yourself in solitude, or to share your feelings with someone you love — a child, a friend, a lover, or a husband. And we hope that you like using it as much as we liked making it for you.

— Peg Streep and Claudia Karabaic Sargent

My Beginnings

I, _____, was born on
name

_____ in _____
month/day/year   place

when my mother, _____,
name

was _____ years old, and my father, _____,
name

was _____ years old. My parents had been married since _____
year

and, at the time of my birth, had _____ children. They lived at
number

_____
address

in _____. At the time,
place

my father worked as a _____,

while my mother _____.

When I was born, my family consisted of _____

_____

_____

_____

How I got my name _____

_____

_____

What I've been told about my birth _____

_____

_____

_____

_____

And about my babyhood _____

_____

_____

_____

_____

_____

Earliest Memories

My first recalled memory is of _____

_____

_____

_____

_____

_____

What still remains vivid after all this time _____

_____

_____

_____

_____

_____

Childhood sights and sounds I will never forget _____

_____

_____

_____

_____

_____

People and places I still remember _____

_____

_____

_____

_____

The happiest memory _____

_____

_____

and the saddest one _____

_____

_____

The memory that most captures what my childhood was like _____

_____

_____

Out in the World

I first started school when I was _____ years old, and went to

_____ .

What I've been told about my early school years _____

_____

_____

The first year of school I actually remember was _____

_____

_____

_____

_____

What I remember liking best _____

_____

_____

_____

and what I liked least _____

_____

_____

_____

_____

How I remember my primary school years _____

_____

_____

_____

_____

How I remember feeling when I was at school _____

_____

_____

_____

How I felt around other children _____

_____

_____

_____

Teachers, activities, and events that left a lasting impression _____

_____

_____

_____

_____

Times to Remember

These familiar flowers, these well-remembered birdnotes, this sky with its fitful brightness . . . such things as these are the mother tongue of our imagination, the language that is laden with all the subtle inextricable associations the fleeting hours of our childhood left behind them.

— George Eliot

When I was a girl, my favorite activity was _____

_____

_____

My best friends at the time were _____

_____

_____

_____

What we liked doing best together _____

_____

_____

_____

How I remember feeling about my friends _____

_____

_____

_____

What I was best at _____

_____

_____

and worst at _____

_____

_____

_____

What made me feel confident _____

_____

_____

_____

and what made me feel awkward _____

_____

_____

_____

I was brave enough when it came to _____

_____

_____

but truly afraid of _____

_____

_____

_____

I remember long veils of green rain
Feathered like the shawl of my grandmother—
Green from the half-green of the spring trees
Waving in the valley.

I remember the road
Like the one which leads to my grandmother's house,
A warm house, with green carpets,
Geraniums, a trilling canary
And shining horse-hair chairs;
And the silence, full of the rain's falling
Was like my grandmother's parlour
Alive with herself and her voice, rising and falling —
Rain and wind intermingled.

I remember on that day
I was thinking only of my love
And of my love's house.
But now I remember the day
As I remember my grandmother.
I remember the rain as the feathery fringe of her shawl.

— *Dorothy Livesay*

Loving, Being Loved

The most influential people during my childhood were _____

_____

_____

_____

The difference they made in my life _____

_____

_____

_____

When I was small, I confided in _____

_____

_____

_____

My source of comfort was _____

_____

_____

_____

And I felt most protected by _____

_____

_____

_____

Dreams and Wishes

...My dreams were all my own; I accounted for them to nobody; they were my refuge when annoyed — my dearest pleasure when free.

— MARY SHELLEY

What I wished for most as a child _____
_____
_____
_____

What I loved to imagine _____
_____
_____
_____

In my dreams, how my life would change _____
_____
_____

In my dreams, how I would change _____
_____
_____
_____

How my dreams were important to me then _____

_____

_____

_____

_____

How my childhood dreams shaped me _____

_____

_____

_____

_____

_____

_____

_____

As I Was Then

How I would describe myself as a child _____

_____

_____

_____

My most beloved possessions _____

_____

_____

_____

Places that lifted my spirits _____

_____

_____

_____

The childhood experiences that changed me the most _____

_____

_____

If I could, what I would say to my childhood self _____

Listening to Myself: Thoughts on Childhood

In our springtime every day has its hidden growths in the mind, as it has in the earth when the little folded blades are getting ready to pierce the ground.

— GEORGE ELIOT

_____

_____

_____

_____

_____

_____

_____

_____

_____

_____

_____

I stepped from Plank to Plank
So slow and cautiously
The Stars about my Head I felt
About my Feet the Sea.

I knew not but the next
Would be my final inch —
This gave me that precarious Gait
Some call Experience.

— *Emily Dickinson*

Growing Up

The first time I felt as if I were no longer a child was when _____

_____

_____

Being older brought these changes in my life _____

_____

_____

Important physical changes _____

_____

_____

How I felt about these changes _____

_____

_____

I was now aware of _____

_____

_____

What had become important to me _____

_____

What I liked doing most _____

_____

The hardest part of growing up _____

_____

_____

Learning and Experience

The most influential adults during my adolescence were _____

_____

_____

What I learned from them _____

_____

_____

_____

Important friends _____

_____

_____

_____

I became more interested in _____

_____

_____

_____

and began to think about _____

_____

_____

The role school played in my life _____

_____

_____

_____

_____

Other important activities _____

_____

_____

_____

Experiences that began to shape me _____

_____

_____

_____

Was I happy? _____

_____

_____

_____

How I Saw Myself

All my walls are lost in mirrors,
   whereupon I trace
Self to right hand, self to left hand,
   self in every place.
Self-same solitary figure, self-same seeking face.

— CHRISTINA ROSSETTI

place photograph here

When I was a teenager, I felt that I was _____

_____

_____

When I looked in the mirror, I saw_____

_____

_____

How I thought others saw me _____

_____

What made me happiest was _____

_____

_____

What I wanted most to change was _____

_____

What I couldn't change about myself _____

_____

_____

I think my greatest strengths were _____

_____

_____

and my greatest weaknesses _____

_____

_____

My High School Years

Where I went and when _____

_____

_____

_____

_____

Did I fit in?_____

_____

_____

_____

_____

New responsibilities _____

_____

_____

_____

and new realities _____

_____

_____

_____

What I learned _____

_____

_____

_____

Best times at school _____

_____

_____

and worst times _____

_____

_____

How I began to change _____

_____

_____

What I'd like to say to the girl I was _____

_____

_____

_____

Loving, Being Loved

My best friend when I was a teenager was _____

_____

_____

_____

_____

What I remember most about the time we spent together _____

_____

_____

_____

_____

What I learned from this friendship was _____

_____

_____

_____

_____

Other important friends in my life were _____

_____

_____

_____

As I look back on these friends, I think _____

_____

_____

_____

Are these friends still part of my life? _____

_____

_____

_____

At this time of my life, in the family I was closest to _____

because _____

_____

_____

The first person I ever had a crush on was _____

_____

_____

The first person I ever fell in love with was _____

_____

_____

My first date was with _____

_____

Dreams and Wishes

I've dreamt in my life dreams that have stayed with me ever after, and changed my ideas: they've gone through and through me, like wine through water, and altered the color of my mind.

— EMILY BRONTË

Two roads diverged in a yellow wood,
And sorry I could not travel both
And be one traveler, long I stood
And looked down one as far as I could
To where it bent in the undergrowth;

Then took the other, as just as fair,
And having perhaps the better claim,
Because it was grassy and wanted wear;
Though as for that, the passing there
Had worn them really about the same,

And both that morning equally lay
In leaves no step had trodden black.
Oh, I kept the first for another day!
Yet knowing how way leads on to way,
I doubted if I should ever come back.

I shall be telling this with a sigh
Somewhere ages and ages hence:
Two roads diverged in a wood, and I —
I took the one less traveled by,
And that has made all the difference.

— *Robert Frost*

Turning Points

At this time of my life, my greatest struggle was _____

_____

_____

_____

Looking back, what I now realize is _____

_____

_____

_____

What influenced me most during these years _____

_____

_____

_____

The experience that taught me most _____

_____

_____

_____

Important decisions I made _____

_____

_____

_____

Learning from joy and pain _____

_____

_____

Within the Family

As I got older, my perceptions of my family began to change. I now saw _____

_____

_____

_____

I was now closest to _____

_____

_____

_____

How I saw my mother _____

_____

_____

_____

and my father _____

_____

_____

The most positive lesson I learned at home _____

_____

_____

_____

_____

_____

and the most negative _____

_____

_____

_____

The sense of self my family gave me _____

_____

_____

_____

A story about my family life _____

_____

_____

_____

_____

_____

_____

_____

_____

_____

_____

_____

My College Years

The end of high school marked a new period in my life. I had decided to _____

_____

_____

_____

_____

How I felt about these changes _____

_____

_____

_____

_____

I was most excited by the prospect of _____

_____

_____

_____

_____

but most worried about _____

_____

_____

_____

Deep down, I really felt that _____

_____

_____

_____

New experiences and challenges _____

_____

_____

_____

Was I happy with myself? _____

_____

_____

_____

New friends and experiences _____

_____

_____

_____

Setting My Sights

Like a plant that starts up in showers and sunshine and does not know which has best helped it to grow, it is difficult to say whether the hard things or the pleasant things did me most good.

— LUCY LARCOM

How I felt during my college years _____

_____

_____

_____

_____

What I wanted most _____

_____

_____

_____

_____

What I needed most _____

_____

_____

_____

_____

Experiences I was eager to have _____

_____

_____

_____

_____

What I wanted to learn _____

_____

_____

_____

_____

What I wanted to show those around me _____

_____

_____

_____

_____

What I wanted to become _____

_____

_____

_____

_____

_____

Moving Toward Selfhood

The world stands out on either side
No wider than the heart is wide;
Above the world is stretched the sky, —
No higher than the soul is high.

— EDNA ST. VINCENT MILLAY

I felt I was coming into my own when _____

_____

_____

_____

What made me independent was _____

_____

_____

_____

I felt happiest in college when _____

_____

_____

_____

and most unsure when _____

_____

_____

_____

I grew as a person in these ways _____

_____

_____

_____

The greatest opportunity I had _____

_____

_____

but the opportunity I missed _____

_____

_____

What I understand now about this time and its importance _____

_____

_____

What I would like to tell the young woman I was _____

_____

_____

_____

Stories That Tell

The story that sums up what I was like then _____

_____

_____

_____

_____

_____

_____

_____

My greatest moment of triumph _____

_____

_____

_____

_____

_____

_____

_____

_____

and most agonizing defeat _____

_____

_____

_____

_____

_____

_____

Other stories that need telling _____

_____

_____

_____

_____

_____

_____

_____

Out in the World

After college, I decided to _____
_____
_____
_____
_____

Deciding factors and influences _____
_____
_____
_____

What I wanted to do most _____
_____
_____
_____

How I envisioned my career _____

_____

_____

_____

and what really happened _____

_____

_____

_____

Personal hopes and aspirations _____

_____

_____

_____

Listening to Myself: Becoming Independent

We are not born all at once, but by bits. The body first, and the spirit later; and the birth and growth of the spirit, in those who are attentive to their own inner life, are slow and exceedingly painful. Our mothers are racked with the pains of our physical birth; we ourselves suffer the longer pains of our spiritual growth.

— MARY ANTIN

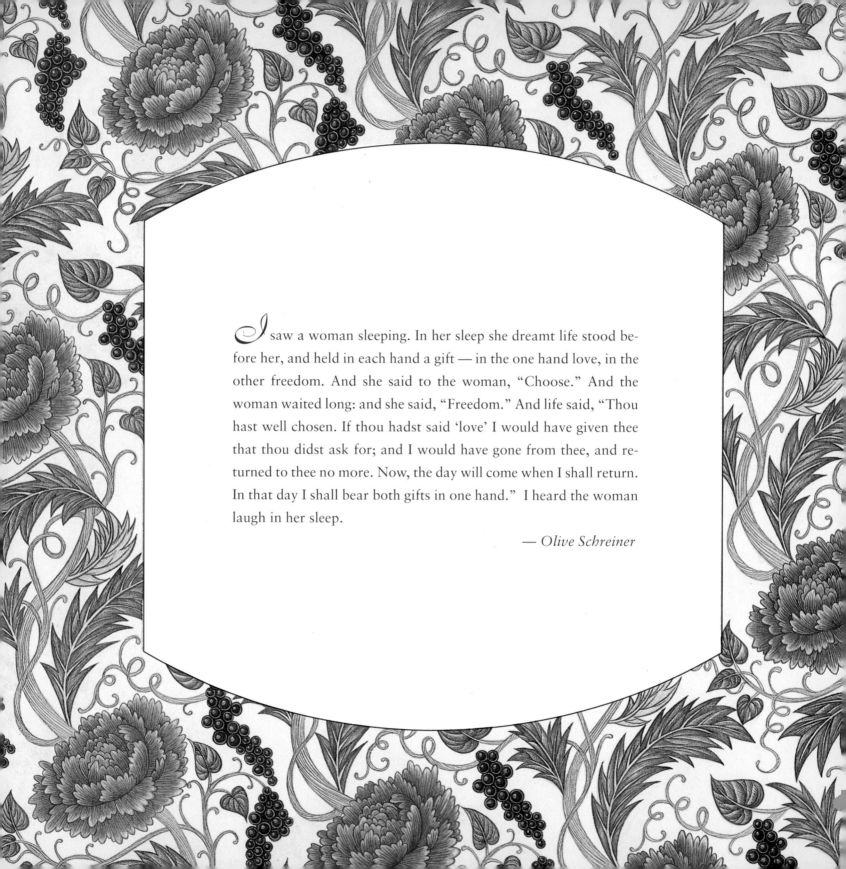

𝒥saw a woman sleeping. In her sleep she dreamt life stood before her, and held in each hand a gift — in the one hand love, in the other freedom. And she said to the woman, "Choose." And the woman waited long: and she said, "Freedom." And life said, "Thou hast well chosen. If thou hadst said 'love' I would have given thee that thou didst ask for; and I would have gone from thee, and returned to thee no more. Now, the day will come when I shall return. In that day I shall bear both gifts in one hand." I heard the woman laugh in her sleep.

— *Olive Schreiner*

The Voice Within

Being out in the world brought new feelings and thoughts _____

_____

_____

How I saw myself among other women _____

_____

_____

How I felt about men _____

_____

_____

What held me together _____

_____

_____ and what tore me apart _____

_____

My greatest strengths _____

_____

_____

My biggest vulnerabilities _____

_____

_____

What I was most afraid of _____

_____

_____

Learning and Experience

The most formative personal experiences of my early adulthood _____
_____
_____
_____
_____

Important events _____
_____
_____
_____
_____

The ways in which I felt changed _____
_____
_____
_____
_____

As I changed, so did my sense of what mattered _____
_____
_____
_____

New goals and aspirations _____

_____

_____

_____

_____

_____

How my work fit into my life_____

_____

_____

_____

_____

How I felt about myself _____

_____

_____

_____

_____

_____

_____

Growth and Understanding

I feel that all the stars shine in me.
The world breaks into my life like a flood.
The flowers blossom in my body.
All the youthfulness of land and water smokes like an
incense in my heart; and the breath of all things plays
on my thoughts as on a flute.

— RABINDRANATH TAGORE

I felt I had control of my life when _____

_____

_____

Important decisions I made _____

_____

_____

_____

Things I learned from times of happiness _____
_____
_____
_____

Things I learned from times of sadness _____
_____
_____
_____

Things I learned from disappointments _____
_____
_____
_____

New understandings and thoughts _____
_____
_____

On Being a Daughter

Leaving home made me realize _____

_____

_____

_____

_____

My own responsibilities now permit me to see that _____

_____

_____

_____

Things I now understand about my parents _____

_____

_____

_____

What I have come to understand about my family _____

_____

_____

_____

_____

Seeing my mother with adult eyes _____

_____

_____

_____

Seeing my father with adult eyes _____

_____

_____

_____

_____

Making Commitments

I knew I had met the right person for me when _____
_____
_____
_____

How I felt about commitment _____
_____
_____
_____

How I felt about intimacy _____
_____
_____
_____
_____

What I wanted from a relationship _____
_____
_____
_____
_____

At this point in my life, I thought love was _____

_____

_____

_____

_____

The ways in which I thought we would enrich each other's lives _____

_____

_____

_____

_____

How I felt when we were married _____

_____

_____

_____

_____

How things changed after we were married _____

_____

_____

_____

_____

Loving, Being Loved

Old friends in this time of my life _____

_____

_____

_____

_____

_____

_____

New friendships _____

_____

_____

_____

_____

_____

The role of friendship in my adult life _____

_____

_____

_____

_____

_____

I think the most important basis of friendship is _____

_____

_____

_____

_____

_____

_____

The people I couldn't do without _____

_____

_____

_____

_____

_____

People I lost along the way _____

_____

_____

_____

_____

_____

Milestones

The most important personal decisions _____

_____

_____

_____

The most unexpected change _____

_____

_____

_____

The most joyous occasions _____

_____

_____

The hardest choices I made _____

_____

_____

The toughest situations _____

_____

_____

_____

_____

_____

_____

and the people who saw me through _____

_____

_____

_____

_____

_____

_____

A New Generation

For me, thinking about having a child meant _____

_____

_____

_____

_____

_____

How my decision reflected my sense of self _____

_____

_____

_____

_____

_____

My innermost thoughts about becoming a mother _____

_____

_____

_____

_____

_____

Joys and anticipations, worries and insecurities _____

_____

_____

_____

_____

_____

_____

_____

Pregnancy and birth _____

_____

_____

_____

_____

_____

_____

_____

*I*f I could only *feel* the child! I imagine the moment of its quickening as a sudden awakening of my own being which has never before had life. I want to *live* with the child, and I am as heavy as a stone.

— *Evelyn Scott*

Children in My Life

How my life has changed _____

_____

_____

_____

_____

Rewards and frustrations _____

_____

_____

_____

_____

New senses of self _____

_____

_____

_____

_____

What I see when I look in the mirror now _____

_____

_____

_____

_____

_____

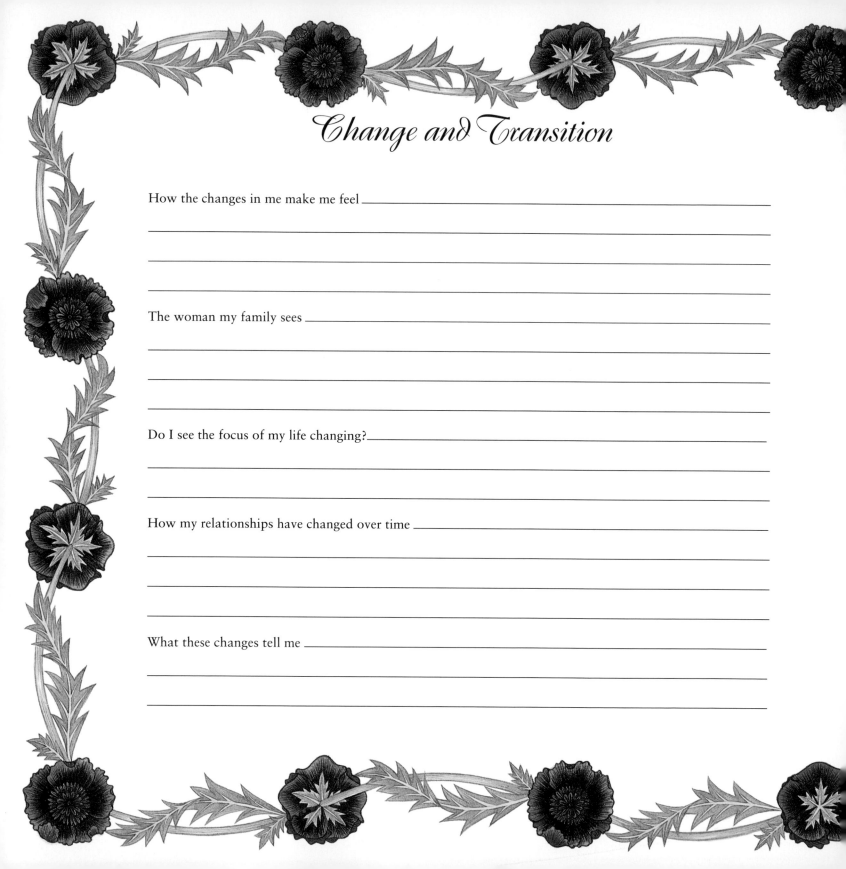

Change and Transition

How the changes in me make me feel _____

_____

_____

_____

The woman my family sees _____

_____

_____

_____

Do I see the focus of my life changing?_____

_____

_____

How my relationships have changed over time _____

_____

_____

_____

What these changes tell me _____

_____

_____

Personal goals I've set for myself _____

_____

_____

_____

Do I feel productive? _____

_____

_____

Am I proud of myself? _____

_____

_____

My sense of how others see me _____

_____

_____

My sense of myself now _____

_____

_____

_____

_____

Turning Points

That shadow my likeness that goes to and fro,
seeking a livelihood, chattering, chaffering,
How often I find myself standing and looking at it where it flits,
How often I question and doubt
whether that is really me…

— WALT WHITMAN

Important realizations and perceptions _____

_____

_____

_____

_____

_____

_____

_____

_____

_____

_____

Ideas that have influenced me _____

_____

_____

_____

_____

_____

_____

Formative events _____

_____

_____

_____

_____

_____

_____

_____

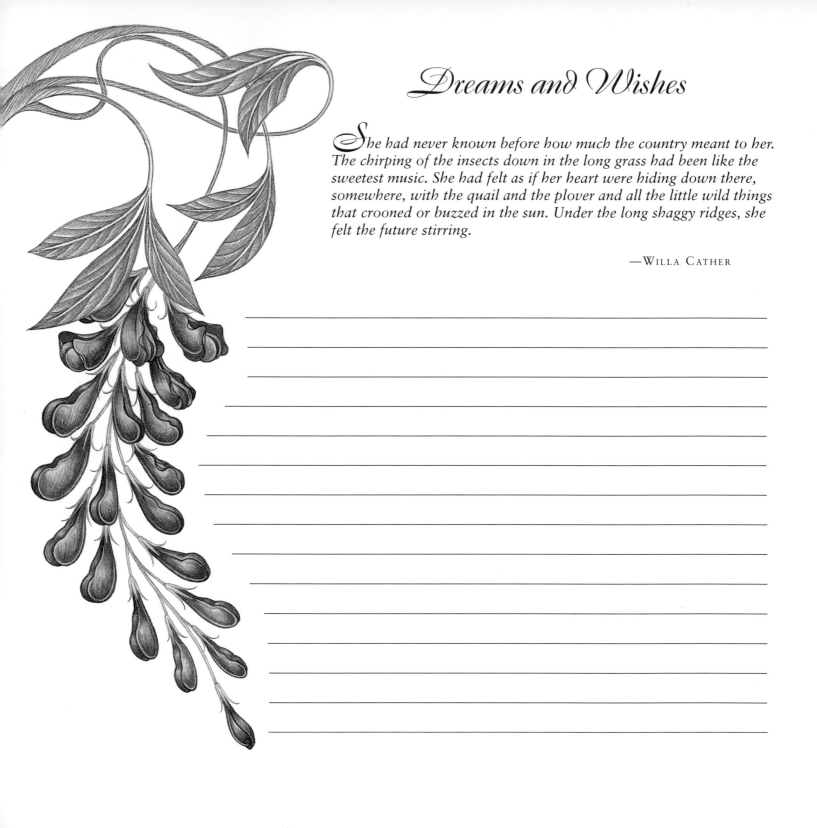

Dreams and Wishes

She had never known before how much the country meant to her. The chirping of the insects down in the long grass had been like the sweetest music. She had felt as if her heart were hiding down there, somewhere, with the quail and the plover and all the little wild things that crooned or buzzed in the sun. Under the long shaggy ridges, she felt the future stirring.

—WILLA CATHER

Yet, ah, my path is sweet on either side
All through the dragging day, — sharp underfoot
And hot, and like dead mist the dry dust hangs —
But far, oh, far as passionate eye can reach,
And long, ah, long as rapturous eye can cling,
The world is mine: blue hill, still silver lake,
Broad field, bright flower, and the long white road;
A gateless garden, and an open path;
My feet to follow, and my heart to hold.

— *Edna St. Vincent Millay*

The Journey So Far

Looking at myself and my life, I feel _____

_____

_____

_____

Things I need to make time for _____

_____

_____

_____

What gives me the most pleasure _____

_____

_____

_____

Aspects of myself still in progress _____

_____

_____

_____

Things I would like to change about my life _____

_____

_____

_____

Lasting Legacies

Looking back, I now see that many people helped me become myself. I owe a

great debt to _____,

who showed me _____

_____

_____

_____

And _____, who was an example to me because

_____

_____

_____

_____

And _____, who taught me

_____

_____

_____

_____

People I never met who made a difference in my life _____

_____

_____

_____

_____

_____

The biggest mistakes I made and what I learned from them _____

_____

_____

_____

_____

_____

Other people and moments that showed me the way

_____

_____

_____

_____

_____

_____

Times to Remember

Triumphs and Disappointments

If you only knew how far short I fall of my own hopes you would know that I could never boast. Why, it keeps me busy making over mistakes just like some one using old clothes. I get myself all ready to enjoy a success and find that I have to fit a failure. But one consolation is that I generally have plenty of material to cut generously, and many of my failures have proved to be real blessings.

— ELINORE PRUITT STEWART

Listening to Myself:
Thoughts on Being a Woman

_____

_____

_____

_____

_____

_____

_____

_____

_____

_____

_____

_____

_____

Looking Forward

Far away there in the sunshine are my highest aspirations. I may not reach them, but I can look up and see their beauty, believe in them, and try to follow where they lead.

— Louisa May Alcott

What I look foward to most in the coming years is _____
_____
_____
_____
_____

What I would most like to achieve _____
_____
_____
_____
_____
_____

What I think the next five years will be like _____
_____
_____
_____
_____
_____

What inspires me most _____

_____

_____

_____

_____

_____

_____

_____

The possibilities ahead _____

_____

_____

_____

_____

_____

_____

_____

_____

Completing the Circle

...of the wonderful stream of our consciousness, what strikes us first is this different pace of its parts. Like a bird's life, it seems to be made of an alternation of flights and perchings.

— WILLIAM JAMES

First Edition

Grateful acknowledgment is given for permission to reprint the following:

Excerpt from *Revolution from Within: A Book of Self-Esteem* by Gloria Steinem.
Copyright © 1992 by Gloria Steinem. Reprinted by permission of Little, Brown and Company.

Lines from "Interlude" by Sara Teasdale from *Lovesongs* (1917).

"Green Rain" by Dorothy Livesay from *Collected Poems: The Two Seasons.*
Copyright © 1972 by Dorothy Livesay. Reprinted by permission of Jay Stewart for Dorothy Livesay.

"The Road Not Taken" by Robert Frost from *The Poetry of Robert Frost,*
edited by Edward Connery Lathem, published by Henry Holt and Company, New York.

Excerpt from "Renascence" and the last stanza of "Journey" by Edna St. Vincent Millay. From *Collected Poems,* HarperCollins.
Copyright 1917, 1921, 1945, 1948 by Edna St. Vincent Millay. Reprinted by permission of Elizabeth Barnett, Literary Executor.

Excerpt from *The Promised Land* by Mary Antin (1912).

Excerpt from *Escapade* by Evelyn Scott (1913).

ISBN 0-8212-2243-0

TEXT DESIGN BY JEANNE ABBOUD

*Bulfinch Press is an imprint and trademark of
Little, Brown and Company (Inc.)
Published simultaneously in Canada by Little, Brown & Company (Canada) Limited*

PRINTED IN ITALY